cleopa
Our Story

VICI McCARTHY

BOXTREE

First published in 1999 by Boxtree, an imprint of Macmillan Publishers Ltd,
25 Eccleston Place, London SW1W 9NF and Basingstoke

Associated companies throughout the world

ISBN 0 7522 1350 4

1 3 5 7 9 8 6 4 2

A CIP catalogue record for this book is available from the British Library

Designed by Blackjacks

Printed by Bath Press

Photographs:
Mike Prior – BIG magazine: front cover, 2, 3 (left),7, 12, 22 (bottom right), 24, 33, 50 (top); David Venni – BIG magazine: back cover,1, 3 (right), 4, 13, 15, 19, 20, 29, 34, 36, 37, 38, 39, 44, 46, 47, 48, 49, 50 (bottom),51 (bottom), 53, 56, 60; Capital: 17 (bottom), 21 (bottom), 22 (top left), 51 (top); Rex: 10, 21, 25 (top right), 35 (top & bottom), 45 (top), 54 (top), 57 (bottom), 59 (top); Mick Greene: 26, 58 & 59 (bottom), Christopher and Gill Livingstone: 31 (top), 43; Tom Howard, 41, Lester Cohen: 42

introduction

hello, this is cleopatra comin' atcha!

We decided to write this book a couple of months ago when we realized that, even though we get to do loads of interviews in pop mags and on television shows, we've never really had the chance to tell you our story our way.

We wanted to write a bit about what we were like when we were younger, tell our fans what it's really like to be in Cleopatra and basically let you into some of the secrets of our lives... so here it is!

We wrote this book while we were staying in a big old farmhouse outside Maidstone, in Kent, where we were filming our telly show *Comin' Atcha*. The farmhouse was brilliant – it was huge, with loads of bedrooms (one of them was freezing cold so we called it the ghost room) and it had a big park all around it with bunny rabbits running around and pheasants flying everywhere. We've never really stayed anywhere like it. But it was great because we stayed there as a family and everyone was there, including our mum, Christine, and our little sister, Terri, who was on her school holidays.

Anyway, we wrote this book with the help of Vici McCarthy (also known as the Interview Lady) who came to see us and help us get all our thoughts down on paper. She's just about as bonkers as we are, and she wants to write a few words here about what lovely, talented, beautiful, fantastic people we are. So...

'I just want to write a few lines to say what a brilliant time I've had working with Yonah, Zainam and Cleo (even if they do fight over computer games all the time which gives me a headache). While I've been with the girls I've realized a few things:

1) Zainam makes great fried egg sandwiches and has, possibly, the nicest nails of anyone on the planet.
2) Cleo is very deep. She thinks a lot, and she's very good at drawing – she drew a brilliant picture all the way through one of our interviews. (It was of a woman with a pram by the sea, and I hope the woman wasn't supposed to be me. That's all I'm saying.)
3) Yonah pretends to be shy when you first meet her, but, don't be fooled, she's actually the loudest out of them all!
4) Cleopatra's mum, Christine, and their little sister, Terri, deserve medals of honour for putting up with the girls' hectic lifestyle.

We've had great fun putting the book together – everything you'll read is straight out of the girls' mouths – and hopefully by the end of the book you'll know everything you ever wanted to know about Cleopatra.'

Okay. That's her five minutes of fame. Now let's get to it. Here's our story, told in our words.

Enjoy!

Yonah, Cleo and Zainam

1 when we were little

This is our story – the story of Cleopatra. We're just three girls who were born in Birmingham and loved music. Even when we were little we used to dance around and sing with our mum, Christine, who was a singer herself. When we look back a couple of years to those days when we rounded up the neighbours to teach them our dance routines, we can hardly believe what's happened.

Reebok

our first memories...

Zainam: I'm the oldest – I'm the old bag. I was born in Birmingham on 5 December, 1980. I can't remember that much about Cleo and Yonah being born. I remember our little sister Terri being born quite clearly because Yonah was only ten then, and I remember her bawling her eyes out. I don't remember Cleo's birth at all – but I was only one at the time!

Cleo: I was born a year and a bit after Zainam, on 30 April, 1982. I remember quite a bit about the others when we were small. One of my earliest memories was when Mum was expecting Yonah. We were in hospital – me and Zainam and Mum – and I saw this lady, Floella Benjamin, who was famous because she was presenting a kid's television show called *PlayAway* at the time. (She's on telly sometimes now, doing holiday reports and stuff.) Anyway, I spotted her, and me and Zainam were looking up at this famous woman, really excited. I said, 'I know you', and we chatted to her for a bit. (Actually we saw Floella Benjamin the other day at the BAFTA awards and I said to her 'I've met you before' and she said 'Really?' And when I told her the story she burst out laughing because she remembered.)

After that I remember my mum going into a room for her scan, and we were looking at the baby in her stomach on the screen going, 'Look. That's our sister!' And it was Yonah! It was the first time she was on telly.

Yonah: I was born just a few days before Cleo's birthday actually, on 27 April, 1984. I'm two years younger than her. I think my first memory was when we were at school and we did a show for the parents. We had to sing this song, 'Chick, chick, chicken, lay a little egg for me' and I was the only one singing it loud and clear.

Zainam: All you could hear was Yonah screeching, 'CHICK CHICK CHICK CHICK-EEEEN! ... '

Cleo: ... and Mum went 'Shhh' trying to get her to be a bit quieter...

Zainam: ...and she stopped singing altogether! Yonah was always the little sister before Terri was born. Cleo and I looked out for her. I remember once she was on a climbing frame – it was one of those Spiderman rope things – and she fell flat on the floor and split her mouth open.

yonah

Although we were born in Birmingham, we moved to Manchester when we were still quite young and that's where we've lived ever since. We were always having a laugh – just like now. For some reason we had this thing about sliding down staircases. Once Cleo and Zainam slid down the staircase in a yellow washing up bowl and crashed into the heater. Another time, when Cleo was only three and a half months old, she decided to go upstairs and then come down again. She threw herself off the top and went shooting down the stairs – flying she was. We don't know how Mum managed it – because she was frying fish at the time – but she managed to run all the way across the kitchen to the bottom of the stairs and caught Cleo with one hand holding a pan of fish in the other. We still don't know what Cleo was doing up there.

Yonah: I've still got a scar on my tongue.

Zainam: And they took me out of my painting class to look after her, which I wasn't happy about.

One of my first memories was when we were doing the nativity play at school and I played the Angel Gabriel (I played the Angel Gabriel every year) even though he was actually a bloke. But as I am an angel, it was just typecasting you see. Anyway, I had to climb on top of one of those wooden blocks we had for gymnastics so I could get high up to show the three wise men the star. I don't know why it happened but my knickers fell down!

Another memory I have is when I was doing ballet and I met the Royal Ballet's Prima Ballerina Margot Fonteyn (she was a brilliant ballet dancer). I was in the papers because I met her. She gave me a badge actually.

Cleo: Oh yeah. I think I stamped on that.

Zainam: No you didn't. I lost it. Anyway, when she died a few years later I was really sad. When I met her she said to me, 'You've got wonderful posture – I think you'll go far.' And now I'm looking up to heaven and going, 'Hey look! You were right, girl.'

zainam and cleo

how i started writing songs, by cleo

Ever since I learnt to write I've always loved joining words together and making them rhyme and writing poems and stuff. Anyway, one day, after we'd moved to Manchester, Mum was looking at one of my poems and she didn't believe I had written it. She said, 'Cleo, you didn't write this. Stop lying. Bring me your poetry books and show me where you got it from.' So I showed her all my books and she saw that it wasn't in any of them and she was amazed. She said, 'So you really wrote it?' and I said, 'Yeeeees.' And she said, 'Well that's good enough to write a song to.'

After that I thought, 'Right. I'm gonna write songs.' And Mum helped me along.

Since then, every time I've written lyrics for a song, I've had to be able to sing a melody to it. I can't write words for a song without being able to sing it first.

when we first got into music...

Cleo: The first thing we did was probably playing 'Horsey Horsey Don't You Stop' on the piano. Mind you, Mum used to sing with us as well, when we went to sleep at night.

Zainam: She used to sing to us in the kitchen. Everywhere. And we'd join in.

Actually just recently we were messing about singing in the kitchen and Mum put the milk for her cereal into a cup and she put the tea into her cereal as well because she wasn't concentrating.

We were always dancing and singing together...

Yonah: There wasn't really a first time we started doing routines together. That was just always what we did.

Zainam: We used to love the Jackson Five and we'd watch them on telly and do dance routines to that stuff.

Cleo: Actually I remember when Zainam was about five and she used to kiss the television screen when Michael Jackson was on.

Zainam: Still do...

Yonah: What else did we used to dance and sing to? Oh! Five Star and Musical Youth and... New Edition. We liked a song called 'Candy Girl'.

dancing in the kitchen...

Yonah: We used to do our dance routines in the kitchen. Did we bump into things? Well, yeeeeah...

Cleo: Well, Zainam used to do ballet so she didn't. She was graceful.

Zainam: Yeah but we used to dance in the garden as well and I had a couple of accidents there. Not many people know this story but I was standing on top of the garden wall once – it was six foot high – dancing to MC Hammer and I just went whoooooo! And fell right onto the concrete floor.

Cleo: I have to point out though that Mum told us not to get up on the wall. The last thing she said to Zainam that day was, 'Do Not Get Up On That Wall.'

Zainam: Yeah but it was a gorgeous hot day though. Had to get outside. The worst part of it was that when I fell, the neighbour's dog, Duchess, went mental. It wouldn't stop yapping for hours.

did our neighbours like us singing... ?

Yonah: In fact they loved it. The neighbours next door thought we were great, but, thinking about it, the people next door to them weren't into it.
Cleo: Actually we thought one of our neighbours was a witch, because her hair was all black with a bald patch in the middle, and we were scared of her. She used to hate it when we got on the wall (the one Zainam fell off) to sing.
Zainam: We used to make up routines outside the front of the house and have the rest of the kids in the neighbourhood join in. We'd teach them our dance routines. Everyone would come out to watch.
Yonah: There was this one time when Mum went out and told us we weren't allowed to go out, but we did anyway...
Zainam: There were a load of kids in the garden all doing the same dance routine – and we didn't see Mum coming back. Suddenly she just appeared out of a car and we all went, 'Uh-oh!'
Cleo: ... and all the kids scarpered into bushes and up the street and everywhere. And Terri was just sitting there playing with a kitten, laughing her head off at us.
Zainam: Yeah, our mate was outside trying to talk to Mum, stalling her, and we were rushing around inside the house trying to tidy everything up but it didn't work.
Yonah: We got grounded a long time for that.

did we dream of being famous... ?

Yonah: Oh yeah, all the time.
Zainam: But everybody does that, don't they?
Yonah: When we were little we always used to watch the Jacksons, wishing we could be like them. Or we'd watch our mum perform and want to join in.
Cleo: I had a lot of dreams when I was younger about us doing performances on stage, or doing interviews, and a lot of them have come true. I get real *déjà vu* about it.
Yonah: And the thing is she tells us about her dreams before they actually happened.
Cleo: Like, when we were in Italy I thought, hang on, we've performed here before. It was a really clear feeling.

what we were like at school ...

Cleo: We all went to the same infants' and nursery school – Rookery Road in Birmingham. But when we moved to Manchester we didn't go to the same schools because there was never enough room. Yonah and Terri went to Oakwood and Zainam and me went to Whalley Range. I hated Whalley Range because it was an all girls' school. It made me sick. There were no boys!

Yonah: I was the lucky one. I went to a mixed school. The only thing I didn't like about it was they were a bit fussy.

The first day I went to Oakwood I had my hair in green and black extensions and all the teachers complained, apart from one. The head teacher said, 'You've got to take those out, they're terrible.' But his boss, the head of the head teacher, said, 'Oh, that's nice.' It was very confusing.

Cleo: I had the same problem. My hair was purple and black, Zainam's was blue and Terri's was red. I don't think our teachers liked it. When I went to school the uniform had just changed and the new one was disgusting: a black blazer – and having to wear a blazer made me sick – white shirt, purple tie, purple jumper and black skirt. And you could only wear black and purple hair accessories. I gave my uniform to my mate, when I left, because she needed it. She was welcome to it!

Zainam: I didn't finish my GCSEs but I'm going to do them next year because I think it's important to have something to fall back on. I did do exams at school, but I didn't do very well – I got Cs and Ds. I'm going to do better next year. Yonah and Cleo are quite brainy though.

Yonah: I got loads and loads of As – even for history which I hated. I also hated maths, which Cleo is really good at. But I'm beginning to get better at it now we're studying with our tutor, Barry.

Cleo: Yeah I don't mind maths. I think we'll all stick at it and finish our GCSEs because they're important. Our mum did a degree recently – she went back to studying quite late – and I think by doing that she's shown us how important education is.

2

comin' atcha

Until 1992 we were just having a laugh with our music. We loved it. We sang and danced anywhere we could, but we never actually made a decision to perform for people – it just happened. One minute we were dancing outside the house with our mates and the next we were doing it for real, in a competition. Here's the story of how we became (de-de-de-deeeeh) Cleopatra and the Attractions!

the competition

Zainam: It's true, we really didn't plan a career when we started performing for people, it just happened. Mum had a friend who came around to our house one day and it was she who suggested it really. They were having a cup of tea or something in the kitchen and we were just messing around in the other room singing an En Vogue song. And this friend said, 'You should put them on stage, Christine, they'd be dead good.' But Mum wasn't sure about it, and she just shrugged her shoulders. Then, at about the same time, another friend recorded Cleo singing in the studio.

Cleo: I remember that really well. We were watching someone recording and I was messing around dying to get in the booth to sing something.

Zainam: She was really small – about eight I think – and the bloke was saying to her, 'Go on Cleo, go in there, have a little sing.' I don't know if they expected her to be that good. She sang En Vogue's 'Hold On', a cappella, by herself. And you should have seen their faces afterwards. They were like WOW! A star is born.

A bit later Mum decided it would be okay to let us have a go at doing it properly, so we decided to enter a competition.

In October 1992, we performed in a contest in Manchester called 'To Be the Best'. We had a live band. Me and Yonah weren't singing at that time – I was shhhhyyyy. I liked singing but I was terrified of the mike. I didn't mind dancing in front of people but I wouldn't sing. I hated, hated, hated it.

Yonah: I couldn't believe that Zainam wouldn't sing. Because she was my big sister and everything and she'd boss me about in the house, but the moment she got in front of the mike she went all shy, and quiet.

Zainam: It's just one of those things. Actually Yonah, I don't know what you're going on about because you were the same.

Cleo: Yonah was terrified of the mike. She'd just walk up to it and just look at it.

Zainam: Anyway, we did the competition, with Mum singing backing vocals, Cleo singing up front and me and Yonah dancing. We were... Cleopatra and the Attractions!

Cleo: Straight after the show I was like Ye-hey! Get me back on that stage!

We won the contest – well actually two acts won – us and another girl. The girl won a recording contract and we won a thousand pounds. Ha ha! Who was the wisest? He heee.

After the show, the people who put it together – Errol Walters and Tony Levell of L.E.T. Promotions – went up to to Mum and said, 'The girls are excellent, they should be doing this all the time,' so they became our agents, and they organized quite a few shows for us around Manchester. And we started doing a lot of performances – in youth clubs and at parties and stuff. And that carried on for a couple of years or so, and we loved it.

Then, in 1994, our mum said, 'Do you still want to do this girls?' and we said, 'Yeeaaaah!' and so we signed a management contract with L.E.T. Management and they've been doing an excellent job ever since – they're the ones that got us our record deal and got us recognized.

Once Zainam and Yonah had got over their shyness with the mike, we decided to change the name of the group to Cleopatra – because we were a whole group by then, and it seemed better. We liked the name because it was original.

Cleo: We wanted our name to be Comin' Atcha actually, but for some reason we decided against it. We sat in the back of our manager's car trying to think up names. We thought up all sorts, but none of them really worked. We thought people wouldn't remember some of them. They'd say, 'Who's that? Bananas in Pyjamas?' So we went for Cleopatra.

But we still liked Comin' Atcha and we thought the two names went well together. So when I was writing the first single, which I wrote much later than the other songs, I wrote 'Cleopatra's Theme'.

Yonah: The trouble is, since that song, everyone gives us a hard time because whenever anyone has a meeting about us or anything, and someone asks a question like 'What are the sales figures on Cleopatra?' everyone shouts 'Comin' Atcha' and the meeting takes twice as long. Not our fault.

our record contract...

Yonah: When we were coming down to London to sign our contract we were so excited. We were saying 'Warner Brothers! How famous.' I was thinking, 'I just can't wait to get signed... that is if they really sign us.' We were sitting in the van, screaming at the tops our voices, singing and everything. We were sooo excited. And when we got to the record company HQ we were disappointed. We thought, 'This... is Warners?' It was just a normal building. I don't know what I was expecting but I thought it would be... different. Anyway, I remember we were sitting in the lobby working ourselves up, saying, 'Okay, we're ready to go in now.'

Zainam: We came out of the lift and said, 'Hi, we're Cleopatra, Comin' Atcha' and then we started singing. We didn't plan to do it, we just did it.

Cleo: It was brilliant. Everyone was rushing out of their offices to see what was going on.

Yonah: The meeting was so boring. It was like this is blah, blah from the blah blah department and she does blah blah blah. And I don't think we were concentrating properly on what anyone was saying. We still forget everyone's names. We're always getting them wrong. We're like, 'What's that woman's name? Is it Katie?' And someone'll say, 'Er, no, it's Sarah.' But still... Anyway, we got the record contract in 1997, and since then it's been mental.

But enough of looking back. We want to look forward! Now we're going to tell you a bit more about ourselves!

3

the 3 of us

Even though we're sisters, the three of us have got quite different personalities. We squabble like other sisters, but we do love each other really and we do get on (We have to! We spend so much time together). You've probably read lots about what we're like in magazines. But this is the truth, this what we're really like. (Cleo: Well, it depends where you're coming from!)

all about yonah...

Cleo: This is what Yonah's really like: Yonah is a moaner, sometimes we call her flonah.
Zainam: She's going to write a song about her now...
Cleo: No, seriously, Yonah can moan a lot. She's got the loudest mouth out of all of us away from the outside world. People who meet her think she's shy, but if you'd been driving down our road earlier you would have heard a loud scream, even if you were a long way away. Who's that? Yonah! She's a foghorn.

She is shy sometimes though. Good things about her are that she's very caring, and really sweet, I can hug her, she lets me play on her computer... sometimes.
Zainam: Yonah is very, very loud when she wants to be. Yet she's very, very shy when it comes to meeting other people. She's very creative though and when it comes to making things, with egg-cups and stuff, she could kick Rolf Harris off his throne. She's a real artist.
Mum: I think you're all like that really.
Zainam: Maybe. I tell you what else – Yonah's very good with her songwriting. She kind of hides away her musical stuff sometimes because if she's got one word wrong she'll go, 'Aaargh!' and scribble the whole thing out and start all over again. She needs to have more confidence in her ability. She takes pride in her work, I suppose. She'll take ages to write three words, like, 'and it was'.

What else? Oh, she's kind of shy when it comes to boys.
Yonah: But I'm straight out if I say I like 'em.
Zainam: Yeah, you are. She's very straight when she's around some boys, but she's quite shy when she's around certain others, ones she really likes, like (shouts) HAYDEN FROM ULTIMATE KAOS!!!!
Mum: (shouts) Or COREE FROM DAMAGE!!!!
Zainam: Ha! She's very affectionate, though, and she loves reading books (usually out loud to me and sometimes I'll say, 'Yonah, I don't want to hear it', and she'll continue reading anyway even though I'm not listening to her).

Oh, but the best thing about Yonah is that we have good girl talks. That's it. She's a nice sister.

what we'd do if we weren't in cleopatra...

I'd like to be a drama teacher, film director, scriptwriter, actress (especially with Robin Williams and Angela Bassett because they're my favourites. Angela Bassett is a real woman!). I like the stage and theatre and television and stuff - which is why it's brilliant that we're doing our own television show. You can read more about that later in the book.

nicknames: fionah, and bullet boobs (because she's a 34DD).

all about zainam...

what we'd do if we weren't in cleopatra...

As everyone, especially Mum, reminds me, I'm very fussy about the way I look, so I think I'd be doing something like beauty therapy, nail sculpting, fashion designing – something of that nature. But recently, all of a sudden, I've got this urge to become a lawyer since we've started dealing with them in the music business. I just think I need something serious to consider apart from worrying about looking good!

nicknames: evnom, lemon... and we called her septic peg when she was squeezing the puss out of her spots the other day.

Cleo: Zainam can be evil when she wants to be. She's got nails to kill for though. Everyone wants her nails, except me, because she scratches me when we fight. That's why I chop them off when she's sleeping.

She has got a nice side though, which is... er... which is...

Zainam: Yeah, very funny Cleo.

Cleo: Nah, she can be really sweet, sometimes. She was wearing my coat the other day and I said, 'You're wearing my coat, Zainam', and she said, 'Yeah well, put mine on then. And now I know every little thing she's got in her pockets. Today she said to me, 'Have you got a pen?' And I said, 'No, but you have, in your middle pocket.'

Mum: What's that got to do with what Zainam's like, Cleo? You're going off on a tangent again.

Cleo: Oh, all right, she's sweet, kind, adorable, beautiful, has a nice figure (hate her)... nah... she's gorgeous. And she's brilliant with music.

Yonah: The bad things are that she wants everything her own way.

Zainam: So do you! Shut it!

Yonah: If Zainam wants something she has to get it. She won't stop at anything.

Zainam: Like that television I want for my birthday...

Yonah: She's a good songwriter, and er...

Zainam: Think hard!

Yonah: It's good to have a chat with her – especially girl talk because we talk a lot about loads of guys.

zainam's tip for sisterly love – don't get a computer!

This might not seem very important, but it was a major issue in the Cleopatra household: computer games. (Everyone groans.)

Here's why:
Cleo got a Sega for her birthday, and everyone wanted to play it. Mum said that even though Cleo was the lucky one to get it, it might as well be everyone's Sega, right? So everyone played it.

Then the Sega got stolen. But Cleo was lucky again – she got a Nintendo from Uncle Dexter, and Yonah wanted to play it (I wasn't really bothered because I'm not really a computer freak like the pair of them). Anyway Cleo wouldn't let anyone play on it because she was being selfish.

Now Yonah has a Playstation, and for ages she wouldn't let Cleo play on it because Cleo wouldn't let Yonah play on hers. It was a huge battle – a War of the Roses kind of thing. And I got so sick of it. In the end Yonah let Cleo play on it – but I'll tell you... it wasn't nice for quite a while. It drove me mad.

all about cleo...

what we'd do if we weren't in cleopatra...

If I wasn't in Cleopatra I think I'd be an architect, because I love architecture and design and stuff. I love decorating too. I've never had a chance to do it but I'd love to have a go. Other than that I think I'd be a producer, because I love music, and if I couldn't write and sing, I'd still want to be involved in some way.

Yonah: Cleo's really weird. I don't know where Mum got her from. She likes pulling pranks on everyone. She's a great songwriter, has a terrible voice...

Cleo: Thanks.

Yonah: Nah, she's got a beautiful voice. Cleo can be really sweet but she can be really annoying too. She stays on the phone for too long.

Zainam: Yes! She does. It's difficult to have girl talks with Cleo because she hides things.

Cleo: No I don't!

Zainam: Yes you do! Cleo's a prankster. She's abnormal. Her face is abnormal, her body is abnormal! No, her face isn't, but her body is. She's really bendy. She can put her legs behind her head and they just sit there.

Cleo: I used to be flexible, but I've got really slack now. I've stopped stretching so much.

Zainam: She's a fitness freak. If she sees just one bit of fat she goes, 'Aaargh', and does a hundred sit-ups. She was doing it in the make-up chair at the television studio yesterday.

Cleo's very creative when it comes to writing songs. But she's very not practical. She's a bit dramatic. You know if you say, 'Oh, my boyfriend dumped me', she goes over the top and goes, 'Oooooh noooo! I can't bear it.'

Yonah: She goes around the world just to make a point. If she wants to tell you she met someone outside, first she'll have to tell you what shoes she had on. It takes her ages to get to the point.

Zainam: Cleo is very stroppy when it comes to getting her own way. Like yesterday, she wanted to go home early and she couldn't...

Mum: That was just because there were some cute guys outside and she wanted to talk to them.

Zainam: I know. She spends all her time on the phone when she's at home, and when she isn't on the phone she's locked away drawing pictures or writing songs. Or she'll be hidden away with Terri, playing with her, acting like a three-year-old. She's a really good older sister. She teaches Terri how to sing and stuff like that. The main thing about Cleo is that when she feels very strongly about something you just can't tell her, 'No.' But sometimes that's a good thing. She sticks to her principles.

Cleo's very affectionate too. She's a sweet sister. We do all have arguments but we love each other.

nicknames: mystery girl (when she's keeping secrets) and scrooge (when she's being mean).

4

we are family

Even though there are only three of us in Cleopatra, there are two more Higgins girls in the band really – our mum, Christine, and our lovely little sister, Terri (who you probably saw, in the video to 'Cleopatra's Theme', stuffing tissue down her bra!). People don't know a lot about them so, since this is our first book, we want to tell you all about both of them.

terri

Terri, who's ten years old, is our little sister and we love her loads; we really miss her when we're away.

The thing about Terri is that she's a mixture of the good parts of all of us, and she likes everything that we like.

Terri isn't in the band at the moment. Mum'll tell you why...

Mum: Well, the thing is, I want Terri to mix with people her own age and I think if we bring her into the music business now she's going to have too many adults around her. She's going to grow up too fast, and I want her to hang on to her childhood as long as she can. The other girls have had a chance – they've been to secondary school, they've done all that and I think now they can cope with what's going on around them. I want Terri to do at least one year of senior school before we consider whether she even wants to get involved in the business.

We really miss Terri when we're away. We've sent her at least a million postcards from all over the world just to remind her that we always think about her. She stays with our aunty when we travel but actually she really enjoys it. The first time we left her with our aunty she was like a twig when we left and then, the next time we saw her, she had a bum and a belly! It was from all the good food.

Zainam: Terri, who's been sitting on my knee throughout this interview, has just stopped singing, 'It's raining, it's pouring, the old man is snoring', to tell us that she misses us too while we're away. But it doesn't always seem like it. We'll call her from Germany or somewhere and say, 'Hiya' and she'll say, 'Look, I'm playing the computer at the moment, do you mind if you call me later', and we're like, 'Oh. We thought you loved us... ' and she'll say, 'Yeah, I do love ya. See ya!', and that'll be that!

Even though she's quite quiet today, Terri usually talks a lot, and when she does she talks really, really fast. The other thing about Terri is that she loves Barbie dolls. How many have you got now?

Terri: Well none right now, because I've lost them.

Yonah: She has actually got two but she hasn't seen them recently because our forgetful manager left them in the office.

cleo, terri and yonah

here's the first world exclusive interview with terri higgins...

QUESTION: Terri, do you like the fact that your sisters are in a band?
Terri: Yeah. It's good.

QUESTION : Do people talk about it at school?
Terri: Sometimes. Sometimes they know when not to talk about it, but other times they do. I don't really mind it. There was one time, though, when their first single came out and I was at school, and something happened. I went to the toilet – just to use the toilet, y'know – and this girl from the Upper Year stopped me and started going, 'Cleopatra, comin' atcha, Cleopatra… ' and I was desperate for the toilet!
Yonah: Sometimes people don't believe that Terri's our sister.
Zainam: They call her a liar.

QUESTION: What's the best thing about having sisters in a group?
Terri: Well you get loads of free stuff from people, like record companies, and you get to meet loads of famous people.

QUESTION: Who's your favourite person that you've met?
Terri: I haven't got a favourite, apart from my sisters.
Zainam: I know who she likes… Aaron Carter!
Yonah: Yeah she likes Aaron. She fancies the pants off him.
Cleo: He likes her too. I found out because I asked him. I said, 'Our little sister really likes you', and he goes, 'Who?' And I said, 'Terri. You met her the last time', and he went 'Oh! I think she's really cute!'

QUESTION: You're in the new television show too, aren't you? How's that been?
Terri: Wi-ckeeeeed! There's one episode where I get bullied by some kids at school, and my favourite bit is when the bullies tie me up to this post with my coat, and turn around and empty my bag all over the floor. Then, when they turn back, my coat is tied to the post but I'm not in it! I get away! I really enjoyed doing that part.

Well there you have it. That's our sister Terri. There's a place reserved for her in Cleopatra, if she wants it when she's old enough, but as she's only ten now she may decide to do something completely different like be a teacher or a lawyer or an actress. Whatever she does, we don't care as long as she's happy.

our mum, christine

Our mum is brilliant for loads of reasons, but the main one is that we can talk to her. She's more like a sister. You can ask her anything about anything and she'll give you a straight answer.

She's strict in some ways. If we ask her for something and we're not allowed to have it, and we push her to the limit, she doesn't start screaming at us. She'll just say really calmly, 'Look, I told you once, the answer's "No." Or, if we really get out of order, she'll just say, 'Okay. Upstairs!' But she never goes mental.

We used to watch our mum singing loads of times when we were younger. There's one time we remember, when she was singing backing vocals for a group at a carnival (Zainam was about 4, we think) and we got up on stage and were dancing around and everything. It was brilliant.

Mum still sings backing vocals for us as well and it's really fun – except when she starts sending us errands to get cups of tea for her and stuff!

Everybody wants our mum to be their mum. You wouldn't believe how many adopted brothers we seem to have got now. All the guys from Another Level want to have our mum, the blokes from Steps, Scott from 5ive wants our mum... she's adopted them all.

Sometimes, when we stay in hotels, Mum cooks for us so we have proper home-cooked food. We lived in the same place for about four months when we were in London and we had a sort of apartment there, and Mum cooked for us all the time, so that we could have as normal a home life as possible.

Our mum is a real nineties mum. She's funky! Sometimes she embarrasses us when we're watching MTV with our friends and she's going, 'Wwwooooh! That's a cool song', and she'll sing along. And we'll go, 'Muuuuum! Shhh!' But it's cool really.

We'd like to give our mum everything she wants – the figure she wants (although there's nothing wrong with the figure she has) – and everything.

Mum: I want the man of my dreams!

Cleo: Yeah mum, but a man might not last forever.

Mum: That's why I want the man of my dreams cause he'll change into whatever I want at the time. And he won't mind if I've got a bit of flab

Yeah, Mum...

If we could wish anything for our mum it would be that she'd always be happy, and that she could live forever.

5 life ain't that easy

Life has changed quite a bit for us since we signed our record contract in ways we could never have imagined. For a start we're never at home, and secondly we've now got a whole new set of friends who travel with us and help us when we're working. People think being in a pop band is easy, and that we just go on *Top of the Pops* and sing into our mikes, before going back to our huge houses to play with our pop star pals and swim in our huge swimming pools all day. Not true! For a start we don't have a huge house or a huge swimming pool! Most days we're working from the crack of dawn until we go to bed at night – and we've got schoolwork to do as well. But we don't mind because we're doing what we love to do. This is what it's really like to be in Cleopatra:

our average day...

Zainam: We don't really have an average day, to be honest with you. Some weeks we could be working in America, other times we might be in London doing photo shoots for magazines, or doing a video or something. Still, we can tell you roughly what our days are like. At the beginning of every day we usually get up and try to have a workout, so that we can stay fit and healthy. We travel a lot and it takes a lot out of us, so it really helps if we can do some exercise every morning.

Cleo: Then we'll have breakfast, and start the day. We might have to travel to a different country, and if we do it's straight on the bus to the airport. But if we don't, we'll have interviews to do – either meeting people at a hotel, or going to a photo shoot for *Smash Hits* or something.

Yonah: At some point in the day we have to study – sometimes we do it in the morning and other times it's the afternoon. We have a tutor, called Barry Withers, who travels with us. We do a couple of hours of lessons every day, and then homework. We don't mind really. Me, personally, I look forward to maths because Barry's a good teacher.

Zainam: Sometimes, if we've had a really hard day – doing telly and stuff – we'll be knackered, completely zonked – and we actually fall asleep in class. A couple of times Barry has just covered us up with a blanket and left us sleeping, and gone to our managers and said, 'The girls are really tired. Let's catch up on this later.' He's cool. Barry's brilliant. He's part of the family now, so really we should be dressing him up in women's clothes and doing his hair and make-up to be one of the girls. Bet he'd love that!

Cleo: We've got to mention our driver as well – Gilbert. He's a superdriver – the best driver in the world. He drives a gold Mercedes!

Yonah: Let's give him a plug. His company's called CIR. The best driving company in the world. We've also got our own van that we travel around in and it's brilliant. It's got everything that you could ever want in it.

Zainam: Then there's Barry and Gilbert, who are part of our crew that we see every day. We've also got our managers – Errol and Tony – who are a real pain in the butt! No, they're really sweet, but they can be very strict, especially when it comes to boys. If we're out and girls ask us for a hug or something, they're fine, but the moment a boy says, ''ere, give us a kiss darlin',' they're say, 'No! No boys! Get lost!' Even if I say, 'Ooooh. But I want to kiss him', they just won't have it.

Cleo: They're over protective, but they have our best interests at heart. They do our security, our promotions – everything.

Yonah: One thing though: they can NOT sing. None of those boys can.

Cleo: When we were in America one time we decided to test them. We sat them down in a restaurant – Errol, Tony, Barry and everyone – and we got them to put the album on their headphones and sing along to it. We made them sing each track, one by one, from 'Cleopatra's Theme' to 'I Want You Back'. I was dead surprised actually because Barry knew all the words.

Yonah: When we first met Barry we were doing the Louise tour and we played the video for 'Cleopatra's Theme' over and over and over on the van, so much so that he didn't want to travel with us any more! Next thing we knew, he started singing it in class! How's that for an English lesson?

Zainam: Anyway, that's pretty much our day. Work, more work, a bit more work, and then, just for a change, some work! At the end of the night we have to go to bed at 10 o'clock, no matter what. We usually have a chat before we go to sleep though...

Cleo: And we scream a bit, rampage up and down the corridors...

Mum: ...No you don't!

Cleo: That's what you think! Nah, seriously at the end of the day we're usually so tired that we watch a bit of television and then snore. That's pretty much it. That's our day.

our van, by yonah

We have a brilliant van, that our fantastic driver Gilbert drives. This van is ay-maaaay-zing! Inside there's everything we could want: there's a Sega computer game installed in there, two televisions, a ten-deck system stereo, a video machine – everything. The stereo's got extra bass so we can turn it up extra loud. It's better than your average home system. We're getting a CD-rom put in there as well. It's like a home away from home – so now you know why we never get homesick!

Keeping in contact with old friends...

The worst thing about our new life is that we miss our old friends. We do try to keep in contact with them, but it's not that easy. The things is we're hardly ever in the UK, we're always in different countries. And even when we are in Manchester and we say, 'Let's go and see our friends now', nine times out of ten they'll have gone to visit their grandmas or they'll be on holiday or something, so we don't see them anyway. But we do try our best.

(Actually we've lost the phone number of one of our friends and we're a bit upset because we'd like to see her. So, Sherena Morgan, contact us! Please call our office and they'll pass your number on to us.)

Zainam: I don't keep too many friends because I don't think it's too good to have lots of friends. That's just the way I am. But I have one friend Chamile – Hi, Chamile! – who has been my best friend for seven years and we've never had an argument. We're even good friends with each other's mums. When I go to Manchester the first thing I do is jump in a taxi and go to her house and catch up on all the gossip.

Cleo: I've got a few best mates. There's Nila Yacoob, Ayan Ahmed, Juanita Coleman, Yhana Ali... loads. I've probably got the most friends out of all of us... because I'm so small and adorable everyone wants to know me...

Zainam and Yonah: Yeah, right.

Cleo: When I went to school I had loads of mates, I was quite popular...

Zainam: (Pretending to sob) Yeah, you took all my friends away from me when you came to that school...

Cleo: But I don't see much of them any more because we don't have much time to go out and because if we went to town, and a fan spotted us, we'd be there for hours – we'd never be able to get away. But I've promised one of my mates that we're going to spend a day together really soon.

Zainam: We know who our real friends are. We know who's going to stick around if it all crumbles.

other things we miss:

- NO Getting Fillets o' Fish straight after school and eating them on the way home.
- NO Sneaking on the buses and trams in Manchester (even though we got caught once).
- NO Yonah's stereo by her bed at home. (Burglars take note: it's alarmed.)
- NO Talking about boys with our mates.
- NO Swimming. (Cleo: Because my hair takes hours to dry and that's no good if I've got work to do.)
- NO Playing outside in the dark with torches (like we want to do tonight, which is Halloween), because if we get our feet trapped in rabbit holes and break our legs we'll be in big trouble.
- NO Being able to have spots and not worry about them showing up on television.

sharing a hug with scott from five

things we miss from before we got signed, things that we can't do any more...

Cleo: Ah! Dating boys! We should just call this section, 'Not Being Able to Date Boys Any More', because that's the biggest hassle.
Zainam: Yeah, we can't date boys because we never have the time which is a big deal for us.
Yonah: We don't get the chance to go to the cinema either. And we used to go to parties around the corner of our street, as well, which we loved, and we can't go to those any more.
Zainam: The other thing is that we've got to smile and get on with it even when we don't feel like it. For instance, if I've got really bad period pains, it doesn't matter – I've still got to work. Mum'll make hot chocolate for me, but if we're doing a television show or something, I'll still have to go and dance.
Cleo: There's not much else I miss really because, before this, I used to be the one who stayed in and read and wrote and stuff... I didn't go out much.
Yonah: Yeah, we used to call Cleo John Major, because she was grey and boring.
Cleo: Look, I'd rather stay inside and listen to music or write some poetry or play my computer, and I can do all of those things now. Still, sometimes someone knocks on the door and says, 'Cleo, are you coming out?' and I don't go, and when they come back boasting about what a wicked night they had, I'll go (shouts), 'Why didn't I go?'.

the boyfriend issue...

It's true that we don't have boyfriends right now, but it's not because we're not allowed to, it's just we never have time. Our managers once made a joke saying that we were never going to have boyfriends until we were 25, and the press picked up on it and took it seriously – what's more they said that Mum had said it, making her sound like an old grouch. It's just not true. Mum said we can have boyfriends now, and we can have steady boyfriends at 18. (Zainam: And I'm nearly 18! Wehey!)

If we could go out with anyone in the world: Cleo would go out with TJ from 3T; Yonah would go out with Coree from Damage or Hayden from Ultimate Kaos and Zainam would go out with... well she's into Scott from 5ive at the moment, or Thomas Jules Scott, who is absolutely gorgeous, oh and Chico Debarge, who is an American singer. She did like Slash from Guns and Roses for a while... but only because he had so much hair she didn't know what his face looked like! Actually we dared Zainam to kiss Scott from 5ive, but she hasn't done it yet. And the most embarrassing thing is that he knows!

We're just like other girls, we've all been heartbroken at some point or another. Zainam had her heart broken by this guys she was really in love with, but he was a million-timer. (Zainam: Yeah, everybody told me, but I didn't believe them and then I found out for myself.) And Cleo got her heart broken by this lad she was really into. She jokingly told him that she'd been flirting around with somebody else – just joking – and he took it really seriously and got really upset. He phoned her the next morning to say it was over. That's life, isn't it? It doesn't matter how famous or rich you are, you still have to deal with love problems.

Anyway, the thing is that at the moment we're all single and we're enjoying life. What more could we ask for?

6

the people we've met

Even though we miss our friends back in Manchester, we're lucky enough to meet lots of really cool new people every day. We can honestly say we have friends in nearly every country we've visited: America, Denmark Sweden... nearly everywhere. Some of the people we meet are famous, like Madonna or the Spice Girls. Others are fans, who always come along to say hello, and offer support, which can be a real boost when we're feeling tired or a bit sad. We'll never be lonely, because we always have each other, but our new friends are really important to us.

the spice girls

We've always loved the Spice Girls and doing their tour last year was really good fun.

Actually the first time we met them was when Geri was still in the band. We loved Geri, she was our favourite, her and Mel C. We're going to see Geri soon, and we'll probably try and hang with her all day because she's so smart, so lovely. She's got a new record deal now and we're really pleased for her. And she's a United Nations ambassador as well. That's just so brilliant, she should be so proud! Her new image is fantastic. We thought she looked fantastic when she sang to Prince Charles at his birthday party. She's gorgeous.

Geri gave us a lot of advice, a lot of stuff that Mum's also told us, like, 'Don't let anybody get you down, you'll be big at first and everyone will love you, but then they'll try and put you down.' But she said as long as we believed in ourselves and did things we thought were right, we shouldn't care what other people said. She said always keep your heads up high. And we'll try.

'madonna doesn't act like our boss – she's more like our playmate!'

madonna

Zainam: Everyone thinks Madonna is our boss but she isn't really. She owns Maverick, the record label we're signed to in the States, but she doesn't tell us what to do or anything. She's too nice to be bossy.

Yonah: Madonna's lovely. She's sweet and very, very funny.

Zainam: And she's smaller than I thought she would be, much smaller.

Cleo: The first time we met her was in Paris. We went for a meal at a restaurant called the Buddha Bar (where Mel B and her husband got engaged) – it's a great place with a huge statue of the Buddha. Anyway, when we first met her (by the way my middle name's Madonna – little known fact), I thought, 'Have we got a connection here!'

Zainam: We just met her in the restaurant and she said, 'Hi!', and we got chatting. We talked about boys and stuff, really. We told her that we loved her video for 'Frozen' and she said, 'I like your video too', and that was before we even knew that Maverick wanted to sign us.

Then we went to America, and we met up with her in LA for the Nickelodeon Kids Choice awards when she introduced us onstage. Backstage she was with this tiny little boy and she said, 'Don't worry, girls. This is not my boyfriend so don't be jealous!' I think he thought all his Christmases had come at once!

Cleo: She's really funny – a nice person to be around. I want to see her again soon – we've not seen her in ages. We've never met Lourdes, either, and we're dying to because Madonna's promised us that we can babysit one time. Actually, that was when we started thinking about setting up a new business – the Cleopatra Babysitters Club – but we haven't quite got that one off the ground yet.

Yonah: That second time we met her she was linking my arm and skipping up and down the corridors and stuff. She doesn't seem like a boss – she's more like a friend who you play with. And you know she's one of those people you can go to to talk about boys as well!

Zainam: Yeah, you can say, 'Aunty Mad! I'm having this problem with one of my boyfriends', and you know she'd just say, 'Okay, sit down, let's talk.'

Cleo: She has given us some advice about the music business as well, but we can't tell you what she said, because it's confidential. She's confided some stuff in us and we respect that.

gemma

Zainam: We met Gemma when we were working in America a while ago, and she really inspired us. We'd like Mum to tell you about her.

Mum: We met Gemma when we were in Orlando, Florida, at Disney's Magic Kingdom. The girls were working on a video for Disney, and during their breaks people were coming up asking for autographs. One girl, Gemma, was from England, and her family asked me if we could sign something for her. Then they told me that she had leukemia.

When I saw her she was in a wheelchair, so we opened up the security gate and let her in to meet the girls. The girls sang for her and they all had a right old chinwag. When the girls had to start work again we took her name and address so that when we got back to England we could keep in touch. We knew she was going to have a bone marrow transplant because the doctors had found a match, and we wanted to keep in touch to see how she was getting on. Anyway, when we got back to England the family got in touch and said that the operation hadn't gone ahead because there had been complications with Gemma's medicine. It turned out that she had six weeks left to live and there was nothing anyone could do about it. We managed to take her out a couple of times and kept in touch with her family, but, unfortunately, she died. Her favourite Cleopatra song was 'Life Ain't Easy'.

Gemma was one of our fans who we met when she was suffering from leukaemia. We'll always reasure the time we spent with her.

hanging out with gemma and her family

Zainam: She really liked the Spice Girls too and we had this backstage pass signed by Mel C, so we gave it to her for her collection. Then her mum, dad and brother came to see us perform with the Spice Girls at Wembley, just after she died, and we dedicated 'Life Ain't Easy' to her. You could have heard a pin drop... Right up to the end she was still cheeky and funny. She really was an inspiration to us.

Yonah: She took the mickey out of herself, and us! She was such a cool person. The first time we met her she was actually filmed for the Disney video, so at the end, we dedicated the video, 'In loving memory of Gemma'. We really miss her.

Our fans are our friends really... we really appreciate the support that they give us. They make it all the more worthwhile.

Gemma was just one of the brilliant fans we've met during the last couple of years. We've got amazing fans – well, friends really – and we know a lot of them by sight. Maria and Sarah in Denmark are just the most dedicated fans. They always come to see us and we really love seeing them because they're so supportive – they really cheer us up. I suppose, though, our number one fan is Richard from Nottingham. He amazes us. He keeps a book with our singles and pictures in – and he'll go out and buy two copies of everything – one for his book, and one to listen to. We took him out once, to say thank you, because he's such a nice bloke.

Our fans become our friends really. Even though sometimes we get hassled, or we get tired, we totally appreciate the support that they give us. They make it all the more worthwhile.

Yonah: One of the craziest places for fans is Spain. There's a radio station called Franco Radio in Barcelona. One day, while we were there, the local people were having a fiesta. We thought, 'Hey! Everybody will be at parties, celebrating. Nobody will be on the streets. We'll be able to go out unnoticed and have a good time!' We went out and saw all these people on the street and we thought, 'Wow! Look at all those people enjoying the fiesta... ', and then we saw a Cleopatra poster and thought, 'Wait a minute... ' Suddenly the whole street was shouting for us and we couldn't believe it!

Cleo: It's amazing when that happens. It's like this rush of energy inside you exploding and you can't wait to get out there. The fans don't just have posters, they have drawings and album covers – everything. One day, I can't remember where we were, there was this one guy crying his eyes out at the window of the van – he was calling me to give me something and I said, 'Mum, if you can get out there would you go and get whatever it is he's trying to give me?' So Mum went out and saw him – and then the guy wouldn't let her go!

Zainam: Some of the fans give us gifts, which is really lovely, but sometimes we wish they'd save their money for themselves.

Cleo: In Sweden, one girl gave us this bear made out of crystal. It must have cost her a fortune. You don't want to take the stuff because you think, 'Look, we've got what we need. You should keep it', but then you realize that if you don't take it they'll be really upset.

Yonah: Mind you, once this guy tried to give us a Playstation and we just couldn't take it. So we said, 'Take it home!'

a special message from zainam

We get loads of fan mail, especially from boys, which is really cool. We love reading letters, finding out what people are up to and what they think of our new stuff. Anyway I want to take this opportunity to put something straight if I can. One of our fans, who writes to me quite regularly (So that he knows who he is, he wrote me a letter with Usher tied up in it! He'll know who he is now) got really upset because someone wrote him a nasty letter and pretended it was from me. I want him to know that it wasn't me. I think one of his friends did it to wind him up. Anyway, I'm sorry you got the letter, but it wasn't from me. I wouldn't do that to one of our fans.

having a laugh with footy star ian wright

blending

Our favourite thing is blending, which means merging with a crowd of fans so they don't recognize us. The first time we did it we were outside a hotel we were staying at, and there were loads of Cleopatra look-alikes out there. We started saying to them, 'Aren't they going to come out?' and they were going 'Hope so!', and they didn't know it was us.

7

been around the world

Before we signed to WEA we'd never even been abroad. Can you believe that? Yonah had been on a school trip to France once, but she went on the ferry, so until we started working with our record company, none of us had even been on an aeroplane or had to try to have a conversation with some-body who wasn't English. Within weeks of signing our deal, however, we were jetting off all over Europe – the first trip we took was to Sweden, Belgium and Denmark, all in the space of two days, and we went, 'Whoa!', there really is a whole different world out there...

Zainam: Our first trips were amazing because we didn't know what to expect. We can't speak any other languages (which is a shame, and we'll be working on that in the future), so going to foreign countries and hearing all these different accents and experiencing all these different ways of life really opened our eyes. And it was weird arriving in a country we'd never even dreamt of visiting before and seeing all these people screaming and crying for us like they knew us and we didn't even know what they were saying.

Yonah: Going to America was probably the biggest culture shock. When we came out of the airport, there were these girls saying, 'Hey! We just saw y'all on MTV. Woooooow. Hey. How aaare yooou?', and we were like, 'Woah. Welcome to America! Is this how it's going to be from now on?' And the answer seems to be, 'Yup.'

Cleo: That first trip to the States was amazing, even the flight there, because we ended up singing for the passengers. We were sitting way at the back of the plane, and fans kept coming up to us asking, 'Can you sing this for us, can you sing that for us?' So we ended up singing to the passengers upstairs, then we sang in the middle of the plane and then we sang at the back to keep everyone happy.

Zainam: Mind you, we also did that on a plane to France too and we got asked to stop singing. Some fans had asked us to sing and so we did. The next thing we knew, this French lady air steward came and said, 'Look, you have ze lovely voices and everything but SHUT UP!'

Cleo: I was laughing my head off. It was just the way she said it. Everyone said, 'We were enjoying that', and the air hostess said, 'Yeah, but zees people are trying to sleep.' So we kept quiet for the rest of the trip.

People say you meet loads of famous people on planes, but we haven't. I mean, we've bumped into 5ive a few times, and we met the cast of *Titanic* once (minus Leonardo Di Caprio and Kate Winslett), and one day we met Noddy Holder from Slade, who was lovely. Oh, and on a plane back from Rotterdam we sat next to Matthew Marsden... but that's about it.

Now we've been doing this for over a year, we've travelled to most places we'd like to visit, but we have some favourites. We love America, obviously, because we've had such a great reception over there. We've done so many television shows, and gone to loads of award ceremonies and stuff there, that it's almost like a second home.

We also love Italy, particularly because the boys there are sooo gorgeous. Last year, we headlined a gig in Milan, and it was completely brilliant. The stage was done up with these great sphinxes, and palm trees, and it looked just like a huge Egyptian temple. Thousands and thousands of people turned up to see us. It was one of the best concerts we've ever done, and we'll always remember the Italians for making us feel at home.

Luckily we've discovered that we all love flying. (I don't know what we would have done if we were scared of it – we spend half our lives

up in the air in planes now.) We look forward to most of our flights even though we've had a few strange *X-Files*-like occurrences on some of them!

Yonah: We were flying from Gatwick to Rotterdam once on one of those planes that nobody deserves to go on – like a box with wings. Well me and Mum were sitting right next to the wheel on take-off, and I said, 'Mum. Look at that wheel', and it just wasn't going straight, it was going everywhere. When we were speeding up for take-off the plane was doing zig-zags all along the runway – and then when we actually took off! Man! Turbulence straight away.

Everyone, our managers, everybody, was shrieking. The wusses! They always say we're scared of everything, but they were complete wusses. It was great!

Actually, I love turbulence. When you're in it it's like being on a rollercoaster, only better because you're higher up. And, if you're by the window, you get the best shocks of your life.

Zainam: Once we were flying to Los Angeles, and were right over the States, when we suddenly got told that we had about five minutes of fuel left. It was so funny! There was one guy on the plane from Manchester who was gasping for a cigarette. When he found out we were running out of fuel he just needed one even more! Mum was laughing at him because she used to smoke and she knew how it felt. He said, 'You don't know what it feels like', and Mum said, 'Yes I do. I used to smoke', and so he screamed, 'Well shut up then!' We were laughing so much we didn't know where to hide ourselves. In the end we had to stop in Palm Springs to refuel, and there were all these cameras outside filming us. We were thinking, 'What are they there for?' It turned out that the airfield had never had a 747 plane on it, so it was a bit of a news story. The good thing was that the airfield was clear, otherwise we might not have been able to land. Can you imagine what would have happened if we couldn't have landed there? Anyway, even when we landed there were more problems. The airport had to find fuel for us, and then when they did, the hose to put it into the plane wasn't the right kind so they had to go and find another one. That was one of the funniest things that ever happened to us, but for some reason the other people on the airline didn't think so.

Like we said, we've travelled to most places we'd like to visit, but there are still a few that we haven't been to. For instance, Yonah would like to go to Japan because she wants to go shopping there and get loads of those little electrical things the Japanese make like spy cameras and stuff. Zainam wouldn't mind going to Egypt, for obvious reasons (because Cleopatra was Queen of Egypt thousands of years ago). At the moment we'd really like to go to that place near Alexandria where they've found another pyramid and the original home of Cleopatra and Mark Antony.

Cleo: It was covered with water for thousands of years and now divers have found it.

Zainam: It would be very cool to go there and think, this is where she was thousands of thousands of years ago. You'd really feel something.

Anyway, maybe we'll get there in the future.

We read about a lot of bands who hate travelling – maybe it's because they miss their families. Of course that's a problem we don't really have to face, because there's always at least three other members of our family with us when we travel.

But, we actually love travelling the world and finding out new things about foreign countries… apart from which we have a right laugh when we travel.

Being on the tour bus is probably the best bit of travelling for us, because it's like a home away from home, and we can really relax. When we're on the bus we'll catch up on sleep, sing, write songs, annoy our managers by putting the music on full blast, whatever we feel like. But we do get some odd things happening while we're on it though.

There was one time when we were an hour away from the city we had to get to and Mum was desperate for the toilet. We didn't have a loo on that particular bus, so we had to stop somewhere. She walked up a hill near where we stopped, and, we don't know what happened, but she fell head first into a nettle bush. We were laughing so hard.

She had our manager's hat on at the time and it fell off into a ditch, so he had to go and try to get it back… and of course, as he tried to get it he fell in too.

what we can't leave home without...

When we travel we like to take a couple of things with us to make us feel at home. Like:

Cleo: My mascot, Nelson the dog from *Smash Hits*. The people at the magazine let us have him for the day when we performed at Wembley Stadium in 1997 and he went everywhere with us, into the dressing-rooms, the canteen – everywhere. But they wouldn't let me have him for good – they'd miss him too much. So I got a copy of him – I reckon it's Nelson's brother. He's Nelson mark II. Anyway, now he goes everywhere with me.

Yonah: I can't leave home without my computer... but I think you know about the computer wars we had so I won't go into that one again.

Zainam: I won't leave home without Mum and my sisters! Terri is actually the group mascot and, if we could, we'd take her everywhere with us, but it's just not possible. We have pictures of her instead.

Cleo: Actually, there's something else I can't leave home without – my jewellery. I'm actually not one for jewellery but if it's given to me by a special person, which some of my stuff is, then I have to have it with me all the time. I've got a ring which is always on my finger unless we have to film, and even then I'll beg, 'Please let me wear it.' It's a friendship ring from someone who really cares about me.

how we learned to do interviews in the usa, by cleo

We do loads of interviews – sometimes about thirty in a day. And I'm not being funny. After a while it can get a bit boring, especially if we get asked the same questions day in day out. In one interview, the interviewer asked, 'So, how did y'all meet?' Doh! I came out of the womb and there they were!

Anyway, after one particularly bad day of it in America, we learnt this technique to get through interviews. Basically we just talk about nuthin', and then after a while the interview is over and we say, 'Oh, it was nice speaking to you. See ya.' Painless!

We realized that if we just rabbited on and talked about anything we wanted, the interviewers would probably get better, newer stuff out of us. So, that's what we do. Talk about nuthin' until they go away.

Once we did a satellite link to America and as soon as we were on we just started singing and talking and rabbiting on, and the American interviewer didn't even get a chance to ask us any questions. At the end they were really pleased with the piece!

So that's our advice to up-and-coming bands. Don't wait for the questions – TALK!

8 the stuff we've done

It seems that we've talked about everything now except what we've actually been doing for the last year and a bit... making records! (Duh!) When we launched our first single, 'Cleopatra's Theme', and then the album, we knew that we loved our stuff but we were a bit gobsmacked at how much everyone else got to like it too. It seemed like just a few days after the first single was released that we were on *Top of the Pops* and meeting fans – it all happened so quickly that we hardly had time to appreciate it...

the records

The first time we went into a studio was amazing. It was when Cleo was about 12, and we recorded a track called 'What You Gonna Do Boy?'. We didn't know exactly what we were supposed to do at the time. For a start, we were surprised that we had to sing separately and record separate tracks, when we'd been so used to singing together. But then when we heard that first song put together, we got a real buzz from it.

When we actually got around to recording our first album we were a little bit more used to it, but it was still strange thinking that these tracks were going to be on our very own CDs and tapes and that we'd be able to walk into Woolworths and see it on the shelves! It was probably one of the most exciting times of our lives.

Cleo: With that first album, we had so many songs stored up that it wasn't a problem getting the material together – it was more a case of which of the songs we would use and which we wouldn't. Then when we realized our songs were actually going to be heard by other

people, I think we all went into overdrive, which is probably why most of the next album is written already! I love writing, me. I can write anywhere – in the loo, in the bath, in the wardrobe, in the shower, in the washing machine...

Zainam: Excuse her. She's weird.

Cleo: Seriously though, I have written locked away in a wardrobe because sometimes I just want to get away and be alone so I can concentrate. The thing is that it's quiet and you can think, and if you've got a song that you just have to get out, well, you need some space to do it.

Yonah: And she did seriously try to write in the washing machine, and we snuck up and shut the door on her. Soo funny. She was screaming, 'Let me out!', and we were just standing there laughing.

Cleo: They did that twice. The first time they did it the washing machine wasn't working, so I wasn't worried, but the second time it was, and I was frightened they'd turn it on. Luckily they weren't that cruel.

Zainam: We had to wait five minutes for the door to open!

Cleo: Zainam and Yonah think this is really funny. Will you stop laughing?

(Ten minutes later)

Cleo: Aaarrgh! Shut up! Can we change the subject?

at the brits

We all love the album but we each have favourite tracks on it, for very different reasons...

Zainam: I like 'The Bird Song' because it's very emotional. It's a sweet song that brings back a lot of memories. It kind of reminds me of old boyfriends and stuff like that. I get a bit deep every time we play it.

Yonah: My favourite has to be 'Don't Suffer In Silence', because it's funky, you can dance to it. It's got a really catchy melody. I like happy tunes that pick you up and get you going. 'Don't Suffer' is great for that.

Cleo: Of all the tracks on the album, I like 'Dying Rose' best. Most of the songs that I've written have been written for a reason, and some of them are about relationships. This was one in particular. It was about when I went out with this guy and we split up. Then, when I wasn't going out with him any more I realized I really did like him. And the reason I didn't go out with him is in the song if you listen to it carefully.

the cartoons

When our first video came out, for 'Cleopatra's Theme', everybody went mad about the cartoons in it, going on about how brilliant they were - and they are, really. It was weird the way they came about. Our managers have always said that we're like cartoons the way we go on and the pranks and stuff we get up to (and we certainly had squeaky voices like cartoon characters when we were little), and it just stuck.

Then one of our manager's friends started drawing pictures of us, and making plasticine dolls of us, and we ended up thinking they were so brilliant that they ended up in the video.

Yonah: I think the cartoons of us are great, because they can do things that we can't. Like fly, and pull every guy in town...

Cleo: To be honest, I don't think my cartoon says much about me, except that I'm small and cute with pigtails. But it does make me laugh. It's nice to have your own cartoon isn't it? How many people can say that?

Yonah: They tried all sorts of different animation before we decided to use these particular cartoons but, to be honest, we don't think they look much like us. Although the clothes are great! And the way they act certainly is like us.

Zainam: They're brilliant, but the ones in the 'Life Ain't Easy' video made me look evil!

Cleo: Yeah, but then you are...

comin' atcha – our tv show

Hopefully, as this book comes out, our first ever television show will be being broadcast in the UK. While we've been writing this book we've been living in Maidstone, in Kent, close to the studios where we're recording it, and all we've been thinking about for the last few weeks is about making sure we do it properly. We've never really had any acting experience before, apart from school plays…

(***Cleo:*** … like 'Chick chick chick chick chicken…')

… and videos and we're really glad that the producers have let us do it. It shows how much belief they, and our managers, have in us, and we're really thankful for that.

The weird thing is that we can all remember our first ever television appearance, and if somebody had told us then that we'd end up with our own show we never would have believed it.

The first time we went on telly was for Granada Television, the regional television network in Manchester. We did *Granada Tonight* – which is a kind of news programme, and we went on to introduce the band and talk about what we were doing and stuff. We were all nervous because we'd never been on television before and we weren't even signed at the time.

Soon after that we became the first ever unsigned group to go on *News at Ten*. We think they did a piece about us because they thought we were a bit different. Trevor McDonald said, 'If you get a pinch of Spice Girl and a bit of the Jackson Five, what do you get? Cleopatra!' We were so excited! We kept taking the mickey out of Trevor McDonald because we really like him. When we ended the piece we all had our glasses on, pretending to be him. We said, 'And this was the news at ten deh-de-de-deh dun dun dun!', but they didn't use that bit. Oddly! We think he saw it though, because he was laughing when the piece ended.

Anyway, like we said, we're concentrating on our own show now. As we're writing this book we've got one more week of filming left. We're really going to miss the crews here – the make-up ladies and cameramen and sound guys – everybody.

So what can we say to those guys, except that the series will be out on telly soon. And we hope that after all their hard work, we won't let them down.

Cleo: The show is all about us as a family and what goes on behind the scenes – and it has some of our performances in it as well. As well as the acting, there's a lot of fly-on-the-wall stuff in it that we filmed earlier. We had a lady trail us for ages. (We called her Raisin cause she was the fly-on-the-wall, and a fly without wings and legs is a raisin – OK, you had to be there!) But anyway, Raisin followed us everywhere – even to Italy to film us with all the lovely gorgeous guys! Wehey! She filmed everything – our daft arguments, messing about – everything, and a lot of that footage is going to be incorporated into it. So, it's a kind of sitcom.

Zainam: My favourite part of the whole show has to be this: at one point I'm at a party and I'm dreaming that I'm an

Egyptian princess and Damage are my slaves... and there they are! They're all dressed in Egyptian costumes and stuff. Boy did I enjoy that day's filming!

Yonah: I get to have a dream sequence as well, which we're filming later this week, and I can't wait. All I can tell you is that it involves me getting married to 5ive! All of them!

Cleo: There are a lot of surprise celebrity guests in it too...

Yonah: Like...

Zainam: Yonah! You're not allowed to give away all the secrets!

Yonah: Okay.

Cleo: But anyway, there's loads of great stuff in it, including animation, and it's brilliant because Terri and Mum are in it too, and it's been lovely working with them.

As we said before, we've never acted in our lives until now, so we're really thankful of the faith that everyone has put in us. We didn't even have to have acting lessons, but that's not surprising because we've always been good at acting up. Especially me. When I was younger I could cry at the drop of a hat if I wanted something. Like, 'Muuuum! Sooooob! Zainam pushed me off the waaaall!' I want a doooonuuut! Sob.'

We've been allowed to make a lot of suggestions for the storylines and stuff. And if in the script we have to say something that doesn't sound like something we'd say, we talk to the director and we're allowed to change it. They're usually cool – they've been really good to us actually.

A lot of the storylines are based around stuff we might do. The television people brought along a dictaphone when we were first getting to know them, and they talked to us about our childhood memories and what we get up to now – all sorts of stuff. They based a lot of the plots on stories that we told them.

If we do another series we'd like it to involve a lot more boys.

Cleo: A whole series of kissing would be good.

Yonah: I'd like Zainam to be in a nice relationship with a boyfriend and for her to be happy all the way through.

Cleo: I'd like to have a full on snog with TJ out of 3T. Maybe get married to him. I'd love to. But saying that, I'd probably die of embarrassment.

Zainam: We'd have Damage back again any day. They were a right laugh. Jade kept pulling his Egyptian costume down all the time because he didn't want to show his knees on television. That was a really good day.

We really hope you enjoy the show, and if you've got any suggestions of stuff we should do in it, write to our fan club. We'd love to hear from you.

the last word

and the beat goes on

Well, it's been a mad time for us recently, as you can see. Since we began to write this book, a lot has happened to us. We've released a new single, recorded a television special – *In the House with Cleopatra* – and done about another million interviews…

We're probably not doing as much partying as we would like, but we're still having a brilliant time!

Doing this book has been a really weird experience for us. It's been really nice to sit down and talk to each other about growing up together – a bit like a mini *This Is Your Life*. We've been raking through pictures and remembering things that happened to us when we were tiny, but it's also given us a chance to look at what we've achieved so far. And we think, 'Y'know what, girls? We're doin' alright.' We're the happiest we've ever been right now, and we just keep saying, 'Whoa! This is what we're doing now? What will we be doing in ten year's time… ?'

Yonah: It would be great if we were millionaires, lived in a big mansion, and had a number one album.

Cleo: You mean number one albums all over the world, don't you?

Zainam: Yeah, and we'd love to have done something with Geri Halliwell as well, because we love her so much. Maybe we could write a song for her or record a track with her.

Yonah: Other than that we do have little daydreams that we'd like to see come true. Like, maybe we could own our own restaurant.

Cleo: Yeah, and a hotel and an airport…

Zainam: I think the airport's a bit far fetched, unless we buy JFK airport in New York and I don't think they'd let us do that somehow. But seriously, I think as long as we're still able to make records, and we can live comfortably, we'll be happy. As for whether we'll be married or not… I'm not sure. I don't think any of us will ever go through with it. We all believe in just being with someone and loving them, because at least then you know you're with each other because you love each other, and not because you have to be. Saying that, you don't know what's going to happen, do you? I mean, maybe we'll get married when we're seventy, when we're really sure of what we want. But up until then, I just don't know.

People sometimes ask us if we'd let our babies do what we're doing when they got to their teens. The answer to that is that we probably wouldn't mind what they did as long as they really knew what they were doing. We'd be more worried if they came home and said they wanted to be a firewoman or a stuntwoman or something really dangerous than if they said they wanted to be in a band.

The truth is that we've been really lucky. Our mum has supported us through what we're doing, but she's never been a 'pushy' or 'stage-schooly' mum. People forget that we come from a solid, working class, Northern background, and Mum has always just wanted us to do well in what we want to do. If we wanted to be lawyers or vets or work in a shop she wouldn't mind, as long as we were fulfilling our potential – just so she could be certain that we're going to have good lives and not end up hungry or unhappy.

We've really, really enjoyed our career so far, and we're hoping that if we keep working at it we'll be able to make records and entertain people for a very long time yet.

We have two favourite mottoes – pieces of advice really – that we stick by and that we remember nearly every day. The first is, 'Don't let people make you do what you don't think is right.'

The second is, 'Believe in yourself and then everyone else will believe in you.'

If we were to pass on any advice to the people that listen to us, it would be those two things, because if you follow them, and stay true to your own heart, you can do anything…